Soliloquies

Richard Mannuell

For Rex, Rebbeca
and the doctors at Millbrook.

Contents

Acknowledgments

I must thank John Keats for reassuring a teenage boy that pain, rage and fear can be conquered through art. Your verse pierced me with a confidence, years of creativity followed responsible for some of my most necessary poems.

Dear Reader,

It is important to outline the relationship between the art and artist before engaging in any of their work. Recognising what influenced a body of work is vital in strengthening the second most important relationship; artist and audience, poet and reader.

I believe poetry is the finest translation of life, of history and memory. A memory can be brightened with lyrics so powerful, the memory is reinvented. This is a warping that reflects poetry like a funhouse mirror. What the imagination seizes as beauty mustn't always be true, if the lyrics are so bold and awesome, then the phycological truth, its brilliance, will justify and defend the poetical truth.

A poem can be tender and a poem can be lacerating but above all things a poem should be fluent, disciplined and unbreakable. It should tax both reader and poet. A poem must be ambitious in its delivery and derived from a place of yearning passion. The reader will easily recognise how meticulous and caring the poet is to their craft and must regard them appropriately. It is a loyalty to greatness writer and reader must obsess over. Now greatness is not simple. It is easier to think what poetry should be than to write it. However if the poet has devoted themselves to an emotion, cause or event and done so studiously, then the reader must appreciate the poets contribution but is not inclined to approve nor applaud them.

I believe poetry is gateless and open to anyone's criticism and contribution regardless of the individuals background, taste for art or lyrical prowess.

I believe creation is a shedding of oneself which allows the artist to develop and mature. The part that dies lives on in the minds of others but the part that remains progresses and evolves until creation occurs again and the cycle repeats itself.

I believe a great poem should unveil a mystery that cannot be explained through standard ways of thinking. It should be as provoking and as moving as the turning of a page.

"A delicious idea comes to me that I will write anything I want to write" V. Wolf

Soliloquies

The Swan

The lake drifts on minding its business
Spending itself among duck and dry land.
It is twilight, the sky unplugs itself,
Loud blue dulls to shy watercolors.
The scene descends perfectly
Like it's been done a million times before.

The aqueous light pierces us,
It ricochets from wave to wave
Into the eye so sharply my hands have to shutter it out.
The ducks bother me as well.
Half immersed in water, copper-coated
Cursing each other out in tuneless babble.

They have threaded themselves along the lake's thin skin,
From grass-edge to remotest wave. Coming as though,
To deliver news from one winged clique to another.
Inland they soar,
Darting across the air then landing unsteadily.
Casing their back with two spearheaded wings.

The swan doesn't partake in any of this.
She deserts the brood and devotes the hour to stiffening her pose.
There is no image more elegant. The feathered naiad cruises,
Parting winds with her aureate neb. Cool and calmly set,
Her wintery sheen illuminates me. The odd jut of S-shaped neck,
Winding and rewinding through ripples and rough waves.

In her mind, the lake is a runway.
Her showcased wings grandly tilted out, her poise perked up breast.
She sails patiently with everyone waiting on her. Joggers pause.
The newborn halts her cry, even the elderly stop their whining.
She isn't stunned by this, utterly heedless of us
She glides onwards, mute as the waters she owns.

The Fox

Our neighbours have wanted it dead for weeks.
Mother does as well
But why have her lifeless?

She stuns me.
Her gold strut across the whirling grass,
The pyramids that mark her ears,

The green birds that glimmer in her eyes
Beating across the garden bed
In search of berries or fallen fruit.

She isn't rare,
A score of them would still charm.
Of all things

It's her nightly prowl,
Nocturnal dive into the wonders of trash
That irks them the most.

We all know it's her.
The subtle footprint written in mud
Belongs to those paws.

But she is so cunningly unseen,
So privately wild,
It feels odd not to admire her mystique.

Pacing and retracing,
Masked by the evening.
Her legacy of

Plastic shards
Dead-bread
Broken glass,

Scattered across shrubbery and
The neighbours newly seeded rosebush.
Her hunger will not shrink.

They are certain of it,
So they have begged to kill it
With a gun or silly trap.

I say she is mythical, almost unbeatable.
Let her melt by the willow
By starling and sparrow.

The Wasp

Peacefully, on a lane of grass
Beside shaken trees,
Soft winds greeting,
Bird wings lilting,
The morning fully ripened
With all tones arriving sweetly.
Then, as random as rain
A sudden fizz, this airy hiss
Began hooping itself around me.

I had no clue
What it was,
It just kept coming back.
This stalking buzz,
Thin ring circling and circling,
A needle through my ear.
I lifted my head
From Hopkins to air
And found two epic wings

Fluttering between my eyes.
She was unbelievably still.
Her gang of eyes, superior to mine
Returned the unexpected glare
Like I had caught a thief, mid-robbery.
Still fluttering,
She hung her pine-framed body
Scorched in gold-lemony black
In one murmurous orbit.

Along the grass,
Over my shoulder.
Along the grass,
Over my shoulder.
Pausing occasionally
Between my eyes then resuming the round.
She went on for ages,
Even once I moved from grass
To elm,

She still got hold of me.
Not just me,
All around the meadow
Families,
Couples,
Children too.
Little parasites,
Swarm of them,
Clowning picnic goers,

Chasing dogs and toddlers.
The air was sick.
The whirring was unmatched.
I had no choice but to leave
The meadow,
Hopkins,
The June Sun.
Leaving with nothing but a batch of stings.
Blood boiled bumps sizzling across my neck.

The Dove

Hollow as a sock
Her squashed breast, flat crest,
Dead wings poured out mercilessly.

The cars are still going.
Ramming and ramming
As dark winds rob plumes, white blooms

Blowing them out like confetti.
The air; spangled with her tint,
Her passing spirit.

She is so unrecognizable it hurts.
The drooping eye.
Bent back bill.

The stainless image warped in blood,
The colour of rust.
And the people, the people just pass,

Passing,
Passing by
Peaceful as her holy flight.

Lily

Two weeks in and she already considers herself an instrument.
Unlearning the nine month silence,
She bells a chorus of vowels.
Each sound drowns another.
She is auditioning for life, tuned in her birthday suit,
The skin she keenly outgrows.

Two months in and mother hones her craft.
Fixing bolts onto bones, shelving garments, goods, bibles and books.
It seems impossible, to carry what will always grow.
Your waking mind; a new hunger to guide and solve.
From room to room, her breast waits like an apple.
You are fed with wisdom and love.

Two years in and our time to visit has finally come.
One rough cough and we spin like meerkats.
Darling, it was you at the end of our prayers,
Your innocence will cover the church.
A priest anoints you
As our keen heads stoop over like shepherds by the manger.

Joy

First light and I wake among your harvest.
Canon of seeds rewarding me growth, a nostalgic rose.
They are the first romantics.
Trading beauty for love, I melt to their touch.

Their passion-tint,
Bright as the bloom that wraps my heart.
Reader, I have welcomed a pierce.
It has numbed this angst and silenced all seriousness.

The air is full of invitations.
Lyrical birds blowing melodies into morning,
Hydrangeas beaming like grounded stars
Along the stone path and the cats melted purr.

It is euphonic.
My garden;
A green hymn
Where I cry and rhapsodize over the world I just turned pure.

Can't you feel it?
Everything undisguised.
I am so light and limitless
I think I may be beginning to rise.

I am only 18 yet I feel enormous.
I feel stupidly free.
God has already accepted my evil.
There is nothing you can say that will deny me.

Saints whisper this, Icarus fell for it.
Reap his gift; the heart's fruitfulness.
So let the mourning descend
As I rise like spring.

Forgiveness

"And when you stand praying, if you hold anything against anyone, forgive them so that your father in heaven may forgive you your sins."- Mark 11:25

Eventually,
Seeking the heaviest words.
The calmest tone.

At times it feels like the purest betrayal.
Shaking the hand that beat you.
Kissing the wound that stole you.

Peeling the words they glued to you that made you feel alien.
It eats you up,
The perfect hate that doesn't need explaining.

Do not be surprised when this restrains you.
Buried with a feeling so deep, you will not answer
Nor heed.

Do not let
The malice of others inspire the malice in you
Else you have lost yourself to an evil you once resented.

Brighton Beach

The horizon is a perfect kiss
Sewn in a marriage of timeless blue.
Nothing inspires its stillness,
The beach spends all day gazing at it,
Wishing it was as peaceful,
As seclusive.

I had pictured this beach day too generously.
A Sun crowns the sky,
Shedding a soft burn on cocktails of bikini-girls
Basking in the August heat.
The shimmer of sea, gulls streaming towards heaven
On whichever route the wind decides.

I'd be lazing on sand; whitecaps unload onto shore
The gush and hum disarming all thoughts.
I could go on and on about how I pictured this beach visit.
We circled the date on our calendar. It was mother's birthday
And we thought, during the thick of summer, a family day spent by
The sea would be a cheap and cheerful celebration.

How misguided we were.
This is not what I imagined.
The bald and old
Scorched to a sour pink,
Drunk on beer and their wife's whingeing.
Buckets of litter befoul the pebble-bed,

Picked up by fat dull gulls who enjoy killing every rare second of
Silence with cacophonous squawking.
It's one of those windless summer afternoons
Where the claggy air clings to your skin
And leaves you feverish and forgetful.

Shade is sacred. Water's worth gold.
We swelter like pigs, boiled to the bone
As a mad heatwave wolfs down children the size of my arm.
Breezes shrink like an unfulfilled promise.

Waves fold and unfold hopelessly.
Nothing booms in this company.

Mother seems the most triggered.
No conversation can distract her.
She sits awkwardly.
Watching the sun retreat,
The evening cast down,
Dreaming the sounds of home.

Granny

I will never be able to cup your voice again.
Your kind words, the ones of self-love and forgiveness.
I used to climb like an ant to the summit of your chest
And earn a bank of fairytales, myths,
Guiltless things which fed the diary of my mind.

I still revisit them
And the moral messages you laced them with.
I remember the long journeys to London,
Across the rural scene and into the hot mouth of the capital.
My eye glued to the window of a bull-black taxi,

Gazing at Big Ben, Parliament, it's gothic arrangement.
Carrying a tray of portraits and poems
I thought would impress you.
I exercise the memory,
For it is too remote from reality.

Granny, your eyes are slipping away.
They are crawling out like an evening sun.
You've outgrown life, escaping the way a balloon escapes a child.
Rising, you rise to a land unmapped and untold.
It terrifies us,

How your charm drifts into nothingness.
These fading days hone the darkest hours.
You must consider yourself a relic,
A bright antique in a world of automatics.
Your Victorian smile, Victorian wit.

Split from your rib, it grew
Grey and unnamable.
An evil thread, sewn like ivy,
Dragged your world into mine.
The gothic voice, the pierce of thought.

I inherited it from you.
Your face is the only memory that burns.
Silent and broad as God.

You will always be forever,
You will always be forever.

Granny, be still.
Let God embrace you.
Let the marching band roar as you stride, stride off.
Grace the darkest night
And let your tired heart rest.

Concern For A Sibling

Love has worn you out.
You've grown tired of the same faces,
The alarm clock and religious objects.

It's a feeling that sours over time.
Soon you're questioning
Every mirror and every eye.

Love has made you weary,
Almost
Disconnected.

You've wandered off.
These years have been a maze,
One big complicated phase.

You've forgotten quite a lot.
Our park of summer, the bedtime stories,
Those parables mother closed our eyes on.

Cold,
Out of touch.
That narrow spark in your eye has long faded.

Nobody knows what divides you.
We empty memories
In search of beauty and your lost voice.

Help us find it,
Help us find
You.

Dear, what silent wound silences you?
What sad voice answers your darkest thoughts?
Let it out.

The pain that fear worships,
Let it all out.
There is a war that hides inside of you

Unallied, you push on,
Reclaiming yourself along the way.
Never forgot how much your needed.

How incomplete we feel without you.
We are always here one door away,
Turn to us.

Album Of Disquieting Memories

Granny, today I visited your old chamber, full of ghosts and forgotten love. Quiet as a coffin, the rooms slept. Six chairs and a king size bed still waiting for you. A moody sun crept in, barley waking up the flowers; the odd rose repeating itself along the curtains. Scribbled scriptures, the writings on the wall, missing words, theories you couldn't connect. I wandered like a child in a museum, emptied a dozen drawers and found a silver album jammed with old photos. How you'd scold me for finding this. My dame, your spirit roams these walls. I touch to unlock. The album opens, I enter;

August 4th 1961- Day at Regent's Park
You are laying on a bed of grass, smiling as an awesome sun turns its eye against your back. Shadeless and probably sunburnt, you gaze up at the wealthy blue reigning over. I read how 1961's summer was unmatched and you celebrated graduating with a law degree by visiting historic landmarks, sharpening the Marilyn walk as you bustled past pickpockets and bigoted folk. Here it says you alighted at Piccadilly Circus, stood and watched the comical billboards burst out their bold phrases strewn above you like a breed of stars. The rainbow of adverts complements your floral dress that billows against the sidewalk rails. Granny, why must you go? You illuminate these scenes but elude us in reality. This image burns in your light, an echo of your life.

November 12 1992- Wedding Day
Her gown beams a dovely whiteness, pearls drape the ears and wrist. Her neck, owned by a circuit of diamonds glinting sharply into the camera's eye. She is lighting up the aisle, Aunt Carol, Uncle Sean the whole church stands as Mother graces by. I read how Aunt Susan handpicked the dress and jewelry from an Italian designer she met in Sicily. After the event, Mother went home helped bake two cakes and ate supper with the family and guests. Father, what happened? upon this day you branded her, swore by the sacrament to cherish her. She was all there for you, tailored up in sunny aprons and fat cartoonish smiles. She was built just for you, delivered like an arrow to the door of your heart. She slipped from the life you promised. Divorce is always the first death, let this image rest as it is.

May 6th 2011- First Holy Communion
I remember this day all too clearly. I'm stood in my row of classmates all dressed formally, smiling mischievously as both mother and father unite behind my baggy suit, resting their hand on either shoulder. I remember giggling as the priest handed the holy bread, winced as I sipped from chalice. The blood red wine sizzled down my throat, I remember fighting the aftertaste for hours. That was life, Christ and my devotion to him. When the mind was fed with fairytales, when the night forget itself so easily. These memories are dead, I must remember that. But they are rising up and holding me hostage. These photos mock me. Their smiles pierce like beautiful stains one could fade back into. I retreat into the memory. I almost envy it, I almost envy them.

Forgotten Bench

Current of leaves,
The dangling limbs of tree
Green over wooden slabs.
Below; along the back.
As though it was nature's mission,
Kindly lost in its earthy submission.

Waiting on the wind

Needy and alone,
The page has not grown.

The garden is brimming.
The winter pond erases itself.

A crow shadows
Everything.

I wait, stilled by the language I learn.
I wait, piecing an image of the promised word.

I wait, to displace the self and latch onto these birds
Or whatever birth the winds bring to me.

I perceive here a divided duty.
I must keep and find myself.

Today, a skeleton of fractured lines.
Tomorrow, a communion of words.

New pulse, the mind overturned.
In the meantime,

I wait for the lyrical firework.
I wait for whatever crowd pleasing word pleases me.

Wakehurst Garden

The hills stride off into darkness,
Tilting the sky with their own unique horizon.
Together they ring the grounds like an arena.
Flared up, eclipsing even the keenest sun.
There is no color purer than the grass.
Endless and omnipresent,
Won by every breeze, their thin heads beat
Alongside the stone path I step towards.

I live here.
Twice a week the fields envelope me.
Flowers offer themselves like gifts,
Promising a world of beauty.
They pour by like rainbows,
A family of colors that graduate as I walk forward.
Bedecking the path, a city of violets bleed out.
Their cruel indigo robs my eye

It is all I can think about.
If I touch their skin I might turn purple
Or be stained with something immaculate.
An oak tree swivels out
A thorny crown.
Its burnt bones dangle an eerie stillness
But fail to pierce me the way these lilies do.
They're unbeatable.

Consider each lily,
Tilting back and forth like a nursery rhyme.
Their clean roots cling to me.
Petal by petal,
I become something pure.
The path rises
Then curves to a verse of roses.
Eager winds sail, blasting the romantic scent all over me.

When the wind blows, it unites all life.
Raging everything in one direction like the thrust of time.

Trees, grass,
The lush pillars that guard the manor
All marry in a mirroring sway.
The manor is the only body that survives.
It's Victorian glow manages to outshine the garden
And strike such glistening tints that visitors wince at the great arrival.

Dark vines worm the concrete plane,
Spiraling into olive webs that creep into
Windows and roof.
Star jasmine,
Climbing moonflowers
Adorn the manor's Midas skin
The same way the buddleia
Adorns the path that will not end.

I cannot complain.
Bewitched by a stern peacefulness,
I welcome everything with unfed eyes.
All day the garden waits like a book,
It's verdurous message has never felt more clear.
The message of the garden is life;
Joy, prosperity and
life.

Midwife at 5am

The cry is a light, loud as dawn. Our voice is a light as well;
Guiding her breath, her breath. New industry,
Her passion dwarfs and defines us. We have fisted her hands,
Cushioned her head and charged the air with verses of encouragement.
This is a ritual, every beat is sacred.

We bustle like wild angels, breathless and selfless
As our journeying hands and blue robes mirror one another.
Making it is impossible to tell who is who.
Calmly, as her cry solidifies, a bold trill beckons and demands us.
We gather like cavemen to fire.

You survived.
Your breath rising, fading into time.
She is love personified; the ribbon spinning a dream into a gift.
Shieldless, she is invited to a world that will not save her.
We close our eyes and bless the path she will own.

I am the elected one.
Swathing her so tenderly,
Her head bulges like an igloo in snow.
I am so scared and cautious, heeding a wordless chant
Then gently responding. Finger by finger I forge the new womb.

And just before
She parts the nest of my arms,
You lean in.
Your stainless eyes pierce into mine,
Bright and hopeful as the morning.

Dawn

Silence
As vast as the sky,
Unlearns it's dullness,
It's dark shapeless body.
This image is somewhat dying.
Stars melt,
Shades fade
As light, the promise of light creeps in
All God-colored and sweet.
Safer now,
Birds unshackle the mourning lyric,
Earliest bliss,
Companion to the sun's awakening brilliance.
Safer now,
The sky moonless, shadowless; unprovoked.
The houses appearing,
The hills greening.
Safer now
The children bounce up; dog-hearted
Solving their dreams,
Solving their fathers mystique.
Safer now,
The morning arrives like a chorus.
The operatic kettle,
Rivers of milk,
The kitchen swinging like a playground.
Safer now,
Her kisses ignite fathers eyes,
Love threads their busy minds together.
Their patient hearts, the ineffable spirit,
Their touch as strict as a sonnet.
Safe, safer than ever
Morning shifts from verse to verse.
Outside, a society of bees argue by the windowpane.
Outside, the young crawl back into their caves.
Outside, An old lady begins her last walk
And up there,
Clouds part as an eager sun emerges like a body out of bed.
The scene cleaning itself,
Bringing a sudden endlessness,

The bloom of heart,
All thoughts revived,
All possibilities stepping forward.
Take it!
A day is born,
Born to be held and sung years later.
The day is eternally youthful,
Seize it!
This is your graduation.

The Rival

Let's face it, your skin is temporary.
Exotic even, a flame in the winters of their marriage.
I cannot name you,
The vanishing touch he crawls back to.

Sunday after Sunday
You have become his perfume,
His silver doll.
I feed off rumors,

Assume what I shouldn't.
A quiet figure,
Mysterious face.
Dear,

I am the child of the one you evade.
The holy one.
She who kneels at the well of verses.
She who calls and calls for love to restart.

Your nudity covers his absence.
Even worse; your commitment.
Follow the fallen
In this game of hearts.

She is more than that.
She is the sum of your religion and desire.
Has forged breakfast and set asters by the windowpane,
Has set the rhythm of day.

Look how she pours herself into everything,
Tending to the kitchen the way a nun tends to God.
It would take an earthquake to shift such love.
You know this.

The ill kiss stains your smile.
How does it feel?
The Parish and the priests are burning, they are burning
Like the diamond ring that burns every time you touch her.

And I saw everything.

On that blurry night,
When the passion fell from your eyes
And you held a knife to her stomach and whispered
Words I cannot write.

Dear,
Reimagine him.
For he has sinned against his body,
He has sinned against his home.

Sidney Lewis

*"It is forbidden to kill; therefore all murderers are punished unless
they kill in large numbers and to the sound of trumpets" -Voltaire*

Father, what will become of us?
Of our lion-heart,
Of the singing in our soul.

They have come in thousands to drain the man out of me.
Nameless and aimless, we march into oblivion
With a nation on our shoulders.

Father, our last summer is approaching.
The dreams are blackening.
We lust for guns.

Hell-bent in this hell-trench,
Where hope is poisonous
And courage is blind.

Voices of pain,
Sleepless and deranged,
Boys blown to ash.

The silence before the bomb,
The bomb before the silence.
Faceless and aimless, we march into oblivion.

Father, what is left?
A lost pride,
A death overheard in nursery rhymes.

His bullet drilled palms
And the nations cross he wore like an oath.
A league of corpses; scorched, severed, unremembered.

So I look forward to the resurrection of our memory
And the life of the world we saved,
Amen.

St Bernadette

"O Jesus, I no longer feel my cross when I think of yours."

She is all there for me,
Lucent among the stone podium,
Her third visit this week.

The villagers think I'm mad,
Take their eyes for they do not see.
Her strange light dawns upon me,

How it flickers and stirs with new intensity.
Like a starved rose to morning sun,
She rises and I with her.

The grotto barely contains us.
Our trance as calm as the cool waters
My knees fold into.

Wisps of ivy eclipse her,
Dangling
From boulders to blue veil.

She is constant.
Incredibly still.
Her soft robes perform a saintly glow.

Her dreamy glare records my weakest gesture.
I tremor, she leans in.
I smile, she illuminates.

If they call me a bystander they're deceiving you.
She has unfolded me.
Polished my eye and named us king.

This is the call.
From Gabriel to her
And she to me.

Unuttered, unexplainable.
It is a silent message
With silent brilliance.

She reads what I dismiss,
Adorns what I shadow.
What I have buried for so long.

Reader, my mind is not alright.
I have come a long way.
Thoughts are thickening,

Senses betray.
Something tells me I'm an accident.
The villagers think I'm mad.

And I fear their judgment
More than anything.
Blinded by guilt,

I have wandered a world; disconnected.
Led a life that does not favor me.
The day calls for my hands,

I may never own them.
Till now I have never felt more heard
And more seen.

No shadow can wreck the light that nibbles at my eye.
It is bold and old
With roaring brightness.

Her spirit; mine.
I am the first of many,
To revel and revere, to spark the promise in your eyes.

Can she feel it?
Does she know these waters shall host a series of miracles?
Seething with miracles.

Her mantle;
A shrine the meek and merry
Shall encompass and revive.

Our Lady,
We will hold you for eternity
And you will always be young.

The future is looming.
There is no foreseeing it.
There is no escaping it.

But
It is
You.

You are the eye that forgives the dark.
Starry and heavenly,
The harbinger of morning.

Younger

Last night I had a dream, it was held by wonders.
Stars roamed our house from floor to flower pot.
In her room, mother slept all day trapped in her own dormition
And downstairs supper made itself, stirring pots like magic.
Outside trees replaced buildings,
The city glazed in green.
There were no bowler hats, no aprons,
All the clocks froze
And children danced on graves.
There was a culture of doors,
A thousand of them, each one taking me somewhere sweet.
For every door I opened, another one closed
Diminishing a light, diminishing a world.
I soon realized these doors were shrinking
And the smell of death bloomed like a bad seed.
O God, keep these doors open.
Do not let them be renamed or reshaped by others.
Tell me, why must death outstare?
His greedy eye creeping in all morning like a vile promise.
It stings, I am no more alive than he is free.
God, let us dream again,
Our future must be found.
Somewhere In a dream where horses fly,
Somewhere In a dream you're never fifty.

Detention

Sir, this room stinks of adolescence,
It's all I'll remember when you kick me out.
This stench, your lousy tie
And the flaccid flowers that sadden by the windowpane.
Remind me why I'm here?
I can't remember either.
I am teaching myself peacefulness,
No weighing scale can measure the boredom we sit with.
We're all frizzled out from trying to keep up with ourselves.
I lean back and manage to capture the skies unmasking,
A reshuffle of colors and clouds strewn across the back-window.
They are so big and unconquerable.
Everyday, ascending
And thinking nothing of it.
The world must be earned.
That summit and the populous of stars.
I have been so lazy,
Picturing myself in the frame of others.
There is a dream underneath my desk.
It reaches up like a prayer
But splits from a future that has no soul.
I don't know who I'm taking to but I know you need to hear this.
The ill stage hones this mask.
We have adopted the script and performed exceptionally well.
The bell rings,
Find your way out.

Laughing Sheep

They gather like children.
Flocked on bliss,
A spiral of innocence

So angelic it seems impossible to get to.
Their lost faces wrap my heart like a bandage,
Like a wish that completes me.

I am trying to distract myself.

All morning, thoughts have been stinging.
Bells fell
And the birds heard everything.

Puffy sirens.
A field of murmurous blooms.
I pass them like a spirit.

October

Gone is the olive blush that sexed these leaves when leaves were fair.
Gone is the gentle breeze that swept the grass and sung the air.

Gone is the viral scorch that schooled the herbage where lush ranks lay.
Gone is the wealthy sky that domed the fields and endless day.

Seasons swing, the sun shifts her eye.

Now a tanned assassin
Unloads her dolorous dye.

The verdurous bed now a sheet of rust
And the world is left to dry.

The Blue Room

So it begins,
The awful metamorphosis.
Person turned patient.
The mind becomes a mission.

Imagine it! In the bleak of November.
A lonely hill where everyone's numb and nocturnal.
The town, nameless.
Our days, traceless.

There was a terrible moon.
Pale and untamable
With four rotten hooves
Galloping a poison so grand it outperformed me.

The moon is
Insatiable.
She is so relentless it stings.
I feel her gothic bells ring and ring.

I am afraid I might transform into something nightly.
Tonight, I unfold,
I exchange my past for peace.
Let the doctors appear like stars.

Fatherless

Child, you are eighteen years lucky and eighteen years deprived.
The sky escaped and you guard a void, a patience
And a plaster that will not grow.

You have pieced him together like the sum of a riddle.
Lost vein, torn wing, a missing pillar.
A crisis so common no one bothers it.

The first doubt is precious.
Reimagining the event in the blindness of faith.
The sky drifts and a vacancy thickens like an image betraying itself.

The second doubt is truth.
Unmisted by their distance and the tired prayer.
The memory is a dream or a curse you crawl out of.

Pocketing that loose knuckle; the world it will terrorize.
Forgetting that random call,
Whatever it meant.

A View From Under The Bridge

Nothing disturbs.
There is only a lake,
A home of grass and this shy roof shadowing.

Tranquil sounds collect us.
The scurry of waves skimming over stones,
Lost boughs in one thoughtless travel.

The lake is oblivious to time.
It sees no greater purpose than to wander cluelessly
Until the image shuts *itself*.

The lake is not inspired by death.
It simply runs and runs quite arrogantly,
Preserving the desire of *itself*.

A duck passes.
Mindless and goalless-
Undisturbed.

Fishmonger at 7am

This is the body and blood.
The body is split, the blood is everywhere.
Cold altar, your silver rusts on the ice-board.
I am here to deliver you from one blue world to another.

You are balding, soon you'll be clear as a baby.
I have tried to make everything still.
The museum walls, intelligent tools,
My soft alb softens this stony sepulcher.

You have held on for so long.
The lab light takes over and the gloves swarm you like termites.
A family of knives,
I pick the youngest one and carve out the parts of you they want.

It is a fleshy maze I worm through.
Pale scales, torn and teased,
Magnified by your eyes Mediterranean sheen.
One wrong turn and I lose you.

The clean glove steers the other, of course I am prepared for this.
The first bump against your bones annihilates me.
Crystal bones, uneven bones, baby bones that fold like origami.
One wrong turn and I loose you.

Glued to the route of vein,
I slide from pectoral fin to pelvic fin,
Hook, hack then slide out.
The high loin parts and the red sea of your flesh exudes its gamy fumes.

I absorb it all, as usual.
Because this world isn't as forgiving.
They cannot hear us,
Your dark muscles rot, I must remove them.

I admire your art, the glow of your gloom.
Pockets of myoglobin, thickened your oxygen.
The battle was everyday.
You and I held on for so long.

The killer waves of the mind dragged you out.
Hung by the tide, I too made the offer and was left to dry.
Last night, I was drowning.
I nearly got through but was coughed out into mourning.

This is the body and blood.
The body is sacrificed, the blood is ours.
Cold altar, we touch and disconnect.
To split from the memory and the world it shadows.

You must go, you must go.
I pour into you, no more than narcissus poured into
The shallow pool which framed a self-indulgence.
What have we become?

They will rename your leaking body,
Propped like a doll in the new ossuary.
There will be markets for your nudity.
Cold altar, your silver rusts on my hands.

The big people are knocking at the door.
I soothe your wounds as we silence ourselves.
Breathe, breathe,
Breathe.

Godless

I am tired of pretending.
Father, I stand by your grave.
The night is heavy.
We are finally alone.

My silence echoes your absence.
Even the birds couldn't worm you out.
From your ashes, I rose. Watered my body
As it bloomed unsurely, learnt the rhythm of your lies.

Carved myself out of your broken image.
The only image of God I recognise.
Your distance shaped me.
Farther, I've outgrown you.

And as I turn and mirror the back you gave me
I feel your quiet bones shiver.
The grave tremors, soil shifts.
It's as if your hands will burst out and grab me.

Farther, If you're alive you were dead then
When we needed you.
It kills, it killed us all.
The illusion was love, that boy is still searching.

Evening Walk

This is the way night falls in the Orchid ward at Millbrook.
The intern, with her fifth cup of coffee, saunters in and
Dulls the radio to a jarring buzz.
My ears fold to it.
We rise and make our way to the quiet room.
This is our home, it has a gothic charm, not as ominous as purgatory
But easy and eerily patient with a perfect sense of order.

The corridor is a tunnel, the walls are wide and watching.
I wander in my fisherman fleece and cross
The nurses office, a lighthouse where lost men pass.
Women gossip;
Horoscopes, husbands, conversations of love.
I smile at the smiling lady,
Wave at the waving nurse.

The nurses track our hands and speculate where the minds heading.
At first I was tense, overanalysed everything.
Now I learn to unlearn, every finger soothes what another suppressed.
The lounge is Leslie's room, a drowned sailor,
Twice my age and twice my innocence. He cruises, blue and bemused
Counting starts from a Victorian window.
Images are toys; the sky a four sided screen that appeared before him.

He smiles, I smile back.
Kindly glowing but still very private is the God office.
Behind that grand door,
A government of doctors unmask the face of cure.
They do it with their hearts, they do it so silently you hardly notice.
Our doctors are concise and cut with a wit as sharp as the poet's eye.
They record and translate everything.

How do we respond?
We simply make our way to the quiet room
And do what is needed of us.
Like a tiger,
Rex strides out the halls of judgment.
You bring me good news from the psychiatric evaluation,
Talking of progress and reciting a letter your fiancée sent.

Her tone's shifted, she's less critical more concerned.
Your soon to be in-laws are thinking of you as well.
They send love and beg you to keep in touch.
You promise me you'll write back and we go our separate ways.
The quiet room is only round the corner.
As I turn,
Night attendants interrupt me and Danny,

A 6ft 4 ex-service man trapped in his 20's.
They hand us each a plastic cup,
Containing olanzapine, the anti-everythings and we raise a toast to our
Girlfriends and the sunnier future.
Quiet as nuns, we enter the quiet room. Here men gather in circles
Unloading our past and stories of abuse.
This session sees Robbie, who's the same age as me,

Retrace the night he was molested.
The psychosis nearly helped him forget.
It was a lifetime ago but the memory is forever.
One by one,
We shed, share advice and reconstruct the dream.
I leave, cool and weightless,
Making my way back to my dorm.

All night,
My brother's cry will follow me.
For every eye that tremors another one tears.
Our fate bonds us.
However painful your experience someone else has endured it too.
The wound is a call.
Not a sickness, a call.

Therapist At 9am

Nothing cures me like your voice.
You sung the worlds forgiveness and brought us back home.
We've tried to understand you, oracle of the orchid ward,
Sacrificing your mind as medicine. Every day,
You rise like a needle and inject your mornings into madness.

I wake, fizzy from pills.
My winter boots squelching through the bleached corridor.
Past the grey dorms and into your sweet cave.
Your office glows like a chapel, a fat crucifix greets me
Between the dream ceiling and your grassy carpet floor.

I enter, questioning the air, the peace lily,
The mob of walls glaring at me as though I'm naked.
There's nothing to distract us. Life drops me in your armchair
The way a cat drops a dead rat on a kitchen floor.
I am dizzy and stale.

Sir, you are desk-ridden among a museum of flower pots.
Fat with intrigue, your silence teases me.
Your diet of short answers and hallucinations has made you insatiable.
I recount the mad nights,
The sleepless nights, the nights that never parted

As you sit like a God, all love no touch.
Zooming from clipboard to keyboard and keyboard to me.
It's almost a hobby.
You unfold a thickening guilt.
"The merciless thoughts are some of the cruelties of loneliness."

Drifting in and out of each other's minds,
To see beyond the sin; you humanize. Our professor, we
The subject being taught on ourselves. And just like students
You acquire from us as we acquire from you, magnanimously.
Some aren't as cooperative,

Exchanging barbed remarks and fanatical utterances
Occasionally leaving your sessions halfway through.
This motivates you, it's the reason you're still around.

You have earned your badge, your crook,
Your odd religion summoning the odd disciple.

I'm still trying to understand it.
The need to retrieve a receding world?
Why take such a risk and why indulge on it?
I'll have to ask you in our next session
Or the one after, or the one after that.

Manic

And this is when the poem begins.
3am; stars twitch, sky switched.
Reader, somethings coming over.
The memory lands like a bomb.
Silence couldn't resolve it.
Thought's run like prey,
These are the meanings I chase.
And this is when I marry the pen,
Every night like a ritual.
It keeps me, not happy, simply keeps me.
And this is the star above the stable
Gliding in and out or dorm with her nightingale torch.
And these are the Greek pills that glow like an eye.
And this is the golden apple that will not die.
And this is the doctor who reminds me of my pulse.
And that is the doctor who reminds me of my smile.
They keep us, not happy, simply keep us.
And this is the tomb I stride out off, unmarked by the terror,
I am no less of a man after, no more of a man before.
And this is the old forum where heavy heads spin and win
Debates, the game of God.
Where the rostra commands the view of a window
And the window commands the dream of a sky.
And this is where I thought the poem would end.
I imagined this poem a thinning vein,
In search of a heart that finally answers.
Instead, the moon bats a thousand eyes.
Blackening; a mind pushed into sleep.
And I am delivered to a night
Cold as the blood that writes.

Arundel Castle

The sky is a skinny pale thread woven in and
Out these seaming boughs like a gothic trellis.
The boughs are harsh and celestial.
They collide and ossify one dark wooden breath.
Risen yet dead like a saint,
The boughs flock and flock an ethereal haze.
White black, on then off. Humans gaze up
Feeling small and lost as a ligneous maze translates a global blur.

This is my kingdom, inbred with itself.
Separated by murk and one huge courageous step.
Eerie spirits tour the grounds,
Persuading the grass and the pilgrim's eye.
The air is royal.
The land is mine.
All day my stony bones announce a rural beauty.
Teasing and pleasing the village that bloomed in my shadow.

My poise is a gift.
Perfect as a sculpture,
Shaved down and miraculously built.
Inside my brick armor
Masses of portraits ignite
Spiraling walls
With fine
Baroque designs

That blend one regal shade with another.
You can smell the fragrance alright,
It hones that grandmotherly scent,
Owning corridors,
The winding staircase,
And lingers in the library.

There is no chamber more gorgeously put together.
The carpet is married to two glorious patterns.
Columns of gold and columns of cardinal red.
Fat shelves overflowing with books,
Old as the crown I preserve,
Sit patiently

Waiting and waiting.
The room, as big as history,
Raised by oakwood, glossy pillars
Mirroring a centuries old glamour.

The visitors are my currency.
With a scholarly eye,
Nitpicking every dent and detail of my body
And whatever ancient myth the tour guides make known.
Of course I envy them.
They come and go boundlessly,
Free from a duty
Of serving and protecting, serving and protecting. It is all I am.

Reader,
My eyes cannot browse heaven.
I am stuck in this wilderness I've convinced myself is home.
Please come visit!
Experience the palatial,
Peerless architecture.
Come and forgive the world
I'm trapped in.

Funeral Of Living Room Flowers

Even the evening's dull tongue cannot dampen such fluorescence.
Nor lacustrine paintings spitting their gaze
So insidiously.

The miracle.
Pretty portent.
Even the wasp continues his hunt.

Even the chandelier spills it's beam
Equally over every bright corpse.
Did you hear what they said?

At the core of my dining table.
A bouquet of lullabies echo the beat of
Heart.

Darling, should these silent eyes
Call for mine?
Should these petaled sirens blare

And ferry me down there?
Child of
Lorelei,

Your dark stars threaten me
To an infinite vase.
Unconscious-unbroken; a dark paradise.

Homeless

"God can never be perfectly present to us here below on account of our flesh. But he can be almost perfectly absent from us in extreme affliction...That is why the Cross is our only hope." S.Weil

Perhaps birds host the eyes God judges us through,
That would explain why he feels so close and so unreachable.
I used to think God was a remedy and heaven; a miraculous scab
That waited like a chalice or a dream.
And I really thought he could see the dimming light,
The odd sacrifice, the nightly prayer

And the mad priest using a bible to illustrate his thoughts.
This is *the innocence*,
Before life shook it and the world blew it back.
You don't want to let go.
The illusions of innocence,
The lack of truth and the urge to uncover it.

Now God floats above us like a winter cloud.
Emotionless and unavoidable.
His stiff eye will not see the gloom,
The dim roof we have retreated to.
The clock strikes 22:00,
Mother returns like a broken mule.

Her stance sickened like a slapped rose.
She prepares dinner automatically, the kitchen clean as an altar.
I am watching her the way Mary watched Christ.
Beaten down, a heart as heavy as the unheeded prayer.
We are so drained,
So unfazed by the need to succeed and want more.

The clock strikes 00:00.
Dinners ready.
She stands over the table,
Fixes a smile and recites Psalm 27:13:14.
We rise then bow our heads,
Roaring the words out like a ballad.

4664

The name floats like a barcode.
The barcode is blue.
The paper is cold, cold as an orphanage.

The invigilators swarm and stoop over us like lifeguards.
They exercise a spooky eye to keep us all in check.
They are not paid to smile, they are not paid at all.

I would like an innocent life
But in my mind it is still 3am.
The pursuit of genius keeps me awake.

It wants to float like a hymn
And stain a church window.
It wants to toil till the point of collapse then rebuild itself.

Nightly it cries, *"We are promised nothing, why are you so patient?"*
I am no more ambitious than the dull circuit
That ignites a fainting light.

On, off
On, off
Someone needs more paper,

Someone needs more time.
Chain of desks, inmate-sweat.
Whimsical pens in rhythmless rhythm.

Darling, we are born surrendering.
But in our minds, wrapped up like a secret,
The dream survives. It is still 3 am.

Costa Adeje

(Written on a balcony in the costa Adeje garden hotel)

The morning high
Sinks the streetlight and raises a sweetness
In the sound of apples, buzzing roses,
The rhythm of eager feet,
Keen to greet the greatness of today.

Sunday Roast

The eye is always fed first.
Indulging on images,
Pools of gravy spill
And fill Yorkshire puddings,
Glazing everything like melted silk.
The French beans,
Sunny carrots,
The hilly potatoes edged in crisp gold.
I am about to dive in.
The chicken breast; slashed
With the plates unbearable screech echoing back.
My eye slithers through a jungle of broccoli
And whilst rummaging through
I catch my reflection darkening at the knife-pane.
My slit pupil,
My teeth sharper than the knife my greasy hand barely grips on to.
I feel like a king,
like one of those gluttonous Edwardians
Blushing in Rococo paintings.
This is what we needed.
Here in the awkward hospital,
Where the minds hunger is always questioned and misunderstood.
In the dreary middle of November,
This heartfelt meal has brought all the autumnal cheer I could ask for.
Danny's thrilled,
He's gorged himself on seconds.
And Rex,
Who has a habit of singing
Whenever he doesn't feel lost,
Has stood up and saluted all the nurses.
It's perfect,
I never thought I'd gather so much from a place so deprived.
Tomorrow, I will welcome the morning
And the sacrament of breakfast.
The air of bacon,
The scorched sausage,
The fried egg bulging with a pocket sized sun.
Light nibbles at the fading dark,
The sky digests itself and by the window,

A hymn of birds shall peck into their bowl of seeds.
All of this is religion.
Every crumb of God will be rejoiced.
We must give thanks to the harvest
And the privilege we feast on.
For there are many who wait.
Children drag their hunger into the night.
Villages that bow to the loneliest drop of rain.
We mustn't allow our privileges
To detach us from the harshness of this world.
Reader, your basics are dreamt of;
Never forget that.
God, let every meal feed the earth!
Let every meal feed our soul.
Here, take it!
The food that isn't shared,
I've heard, goes off!

Daydreaming

Blue bulb, black bulb,
The ceiling is leaking
A cold light.
Doctor, I'm in a bit of a fright.
The glue on this chair is melting.
The pins are loosening.
Am I being too needy?
Three rounds in and I still flinch at the flash of your needles.
Your shepherd eye, clean as a midwife,
Follows my blood as it blooms in tubes,
Who knew your magic would unleash mine.
I lean back and guess the weather
As your measurements flock together.

Grey bulb, foggy bulb,
The ceiling is leaking
A cold light.
Doctor, please do not lie.
Will it hurt when they scrap the mould of my mind?
I am not prepared to accept.
You open my hand like an oyster.
Your knowledge round and rare.
The white wards wait on your ringmaster hands
To reel us into whatever realness we had.
I lean back and revisit my Grandmother.
Your dark scarfs and missing eye.
I cried in your lap as you rocked from one world to another.

Split bulb, fizzy bulb,
The ceiling is leaking
A cold light.
Doctor, how old is your might?
There is a grand row of black and white photos.
Royal banners, diplomas, hanging like haloes.
To dazzle in the web of your intellect.
A generational bow, I don't think you need more polishing.
You will find me at the heart of the labyrinth.
Peeling and kneeling to a nursing pen.

Yes, that's right. Your practise is *the poem*.
Where the fate written is not the fate dealt,
Where the last word said isn't the last word felt.

The Mannequin

Today I crack open like a scab
Or a pair of stale wings.
The hands are specific, a face plain as clay

And my window; a silent dome
That keeps the vivarium approachable.
Bright cell, easy stranger. We count them like coins.

They have traded our skin for doll eyes and
Advertised clothes.
Petalous, we invite you.

Mirrors tease a blind desire;
A dependency of faults
Guiding your fears of becoming unpopular.

Lights on and our life becomes a pose
In conversation with eyes, negotiating eyes.
I can't explain the feeling and I don't have to.

Our call is a reverie;
A framed wish hung like Ivory.
Illusory, we wait.

"I am not perfect though I wish I was symmetrical"

Each corpse itemises your needs,
The need to make a connection.
In vogue or in vain, you need to make a connection.

Mirrors turn and I absorb a distance.
This is the final image.
The image; a rose you dissect,

The self; unexpressed.
These materials cannot guard a body that isn't home.
Bone at my bone; an ornamental growth.

Lights off and life becomes a question,
A taming of thoughts.
Beauty is taxing,

How you spend and mend yourself so cruelly.
Soulless minds, mindless eyes.
I am surviving on the outside.

Like a moth, you arrive at a lethal intrigue.
To adjust an eye
And confuse the performance I was groomed into.

By noon, we will have purchased your hand.
Covered and corrupt,
Tangled up like a poem.

Soliloquy

Fever,
Fever of voices
Seethe and breed a great secret.

Something went off.
A discolouring.
Slow as rust; a weak reply.

Blue mirror,
Sudden absence,
A traumatised heart.

Darling why didn't you call,
How have we been so patient?
Something went off.

In the prison of himself,
In the strangle of fate,
Sense made nothing and nothing feels sincere.

Patience.
A bottled man
Emptied of dreams.

I am left with the hunger of walls,
The thrill of eyes,
A circus of thoughts.

The radio bleeds,
Memories lie and bicker over screen time.
Barred windows daubed with moss

And a loose wallpaper faulted by lines,
Vertiginous lines; writhing then
Ricocheting one another.

The lines are not futureless, they want to get out.
But at every ambitious curve they trip,
Fall and abandon themselves in torturous patterns,

Shapes that sin and bleed into one another.
One stooping line quivers and stares right at me like a dead pupil.
Angry and powerless; a fish out of water.

There are things in this wall nobody hears but me.
Behind those patterns a dim figure, pressed into silence,
Echos something left unsaid.

I believe he is stuck and brutally forgotten.
like flotsam, he is switched off.
I believe he doesn't believe in himself.

All night, my light tends to their spirit.
The isthmus; the bridging voice.
Our shadows merge and the lines are beginning to blur.

Something went off.
You carry shame like a gun.
That fear corners truth, the ripening inside of you.

Should the truth threaten you?
Why should it burn and burn like a fever,
A great secret.

The Untouchable Women

*"It will perhaps appear to them, that wishing to avoid the prevalent
fault of day, the author has sometimes descended too low, and that
many of his expressions are too familiar and not of sufficient dignity"*
 -W. Wordsworth

They cannot imagine me, I imagine them.
I was 12 when I first met them. Young and dopamine driven, I wanted
to soothe that libidinous itch. I didn't realise it but on that day I opened
a world of nudity, stainless women at the click of my finger. It's a weird
type of surrendering, to command a presence you fully submit to.
I am not your typical catholic and this is not your typical sin; these
gorgons got me.

And, yes, I admit it's become a habit. Nightly, sometimes hourly,
I fall Into it. Some say its self-love; a fast spark for a dead heart. An
insomniac trying to cloud their restless thoughts. Reader, I'm dreaming
of skin, the intimacy of her and her, her and her. Intertwined, their
touch sparks mine. These vamps demonstrate what I lack.

I respond, of course, it's my way out. The lonely caress ends with a
lonely thrill then the heaviest guilt returns. And yes we abstain, try to
abstain but the night stalls and before you can numb the feeling a
hunger calls, strict and selfless; it wants us to cope.

Garden Of November

"The grave empty and the stone rolled away... they realised the new wonder; but even they hardly realised that the world had died in the night" -G.K Chesterton .

It was only a door I had lost or a root I had pulled.
The rooms of the mind are lightless.
A blurred space that waits like a seed.

Patience, the cost can be lethal.
Is this the world I wanted?
Here, in my brown orbit of love

Where the sin has dried and dimmed.
The garden descends.
A deciduous response of gold.

Picture it.
The crunch and kiss of foliage as I push and part new winds.
The sun, quiet as a tomb.

I have found the Motherbox.
The cornucopia overflows with poetry.
Ashes turn, my faith burns, to bury and become.

Winter anoints the annual death.
The emerald ray breaks.
The trees have alopecia

And the meadows are being skinned alive.
A message sewn through boughs,
These shifting boughs.

They cannot hide what hope couldn't save.
They let go.
A change of home.

We can finally breathe.
There is a death in freedom,
In escaping a futureless past.

Reader, we have come so far.
Do not look back,
Do not look back.

In Spite Of Cruelty

Because I thought it was foolish,
Undermined everything in fear of conversion.
I unlearnt.

Caught my prayer and swallowed it.
Fled your merciless eye,
Fled my Father's philosophy.

In fact, I thought it was necessary.
Assuming freedom was a belief not an outcome.
Assuming the misguided somehow find themselves.

In my strange world love was out of range
And I could not face nor forgive myself.
Cold angels addressed me.

Murmuring ills,
Songs of guilt.
Still thought it was foolish.

Turned stoic
As the season of youth passed,
As the quiet storm grew over me.

Then came the order of doctors, the routine of scriptures.
Hours poured in the confessional cabinet,
Digging out the ruin, the buried sin.

Beardless prophets gave lyric to the unspeakable.
Admitting the wound was more painful than its infliction.
Still I dug, through warm interrogations,

To uncover the unsaid.
I left the scene
With a heart full of poems.

Each one bottling a light,
A delivering light.
I wrote till I was blind.

I couldn't distort the truth,
I journeyed with it.
Armed with faith, I bring you good news.

All along
I feared fate,
My furious doubt,

Thinking I was irredeemable.
All along,
I mistook this journey.

Reader, nothing is promised to us.
Each day is a climb,
A mountainous build.

And at the summit of our choices
We stare and reflect
Remembering who we are and where we're needed.

The name you kill but never say is mine.
The journey is discipline, the discipline is life.
I am not living for myself I am living for the man I must become.

For the old man parting clouds,
For the bride who waits like a birthday,
For the band of tongues that rose against us.

Yesterday's lesson built the steps of today.
I ascend,
Tomorrow is paradise.

Coroner At 3pm

If sin took figure it would be unrecognisable, yet here she is.
"Mary Jane Kelly", her body discovered yesterday at 10:45am.
I first caught wind of the event this afternoon, one of the officers
informed me on a homicide, the fifth of its kind.
"We still aint got a clue who done it". Their lack of knowledge is what's
really getting to me.

Not just the senseless killings tallying up but the faceless perpetrator
behind them. I was dispatched at around 14:00pm, allied with
detectives and a herd of reporters. Our destination was a dimly lit
unfurnished single room at the end of Dorsey street. We arrived at the
scene expecting the usual but what we witnessed was something
unimaginable; an episode of rage.

Shreds of flesh litter the blood drenched bed. Veins, wet veins, blue
veins dangle from the hell-ceiling. It's a freak show. I take one step and
wheeze as my feet squeeze on warm viscera. A drizzling red surfs the
wall that shadows the disembowelled. That's her, emptied out like a
plastic bag, like gralloch. The detectives won't even look, you can't
blame them.

The sight is annihilating. Her face disfeatured, her mouth cries open.
Her hair draggled, curdled with blood clots, dark and icky as caramel.
Her skin, minced, slit, gashed with a bewildering number of bruises
and gooey scars. The carcass mottles the bed she rots on. I squat like a
vet inspecting the mauled and mangled remains while detectives scour
the pigsty.

Carefully unlocking pieces of evidence. We're half-numb, half-eager to
solve this case and identify the sicko who's responsible for this.
A vulturous lust dragged him to this crime. He is nameless, last night
he polished his scythe and made himself popular; magazine worthy.
Whitechapel can't get enough of him, neither can we.

This death is performance, it is arrogant and pretentious. A crescent of
heads peer over.
"Maybe she's a pacifist," an officer murmured.
"Maybe what he purchased isn't what she promised," another snarked.
The horror's so vivid it's made her life seem meaningless.

She's become public domain.
They'll bury the odd limbs in silver jars hung up in some strange
museum. Spectators will pour, the town dulls to a passing silence
and the hysterical ones will shriek at this marvel
then move on,
as the event shrinks to a memory of forgotten violence.

Study Of A Yew Tree

Posing in the murk of St. John's church,
A gothic flamboyance
Shadows my foot, the unwinding path.
He is unspoken
And I, with quiet amazement, stand before him.

He has gathered a perverted shape.
Unevenly flocked a fortress of limbs.
Strange thing,
No other gravely figure allures me.
I cannot translate his mystique,

Nor trace his history, all I greet is an aimless bloom
That spirals into eternal oblivion.
His serpent hair owes its mad fashion
To ranks of erratic thorns, arranging, then
Rearranging themselves in angry columns above my skull.

His sunless foot circled by a disc of ash,
His brute trunk tipped like an ancient pillar.
His doom-skin, tough as a Celtic shield,
Pours a funereal glow interrupting daylight,
Those hymns and hourly bells.

Even the headstones, flocked like Cardinals to a Pope,
Tilt back in fear of his kingliness.
His splintered crown and plutonian skirts.
No one can deny him.
Cold spirits tremor beneath those boughs,

Soulless voices,
A sinister call.
I'm afraid I may join the unheard.
They say he doesn't believe in heaven.
Uninspired by

Time,
For he is produced too slowly to ever decay.
I wish to sing that peace.

To face the abyss yet never expect it,
To wither and ascend though never truly cease.

To Dr Lawson Who Wishes To Cage My Pen

"Do you not see how necessary a world of pains
and troubles is, to school an intelligence and make it a soul." J. Keats

Sir, my mind is a business, a market of words. It doesn't cost much,
demanding only a pen and a surrendering table. Usually, the words
find themselves flocking together like clever sheep. Very quick, very
sincere but very docile, easy to manipulate. Every word uncovers
another that hints towards something I may or may have not said.
Eventually you have a swarm of meanings unique to you entirely made
up by yourself. Don't blame me for this, the second you descend into
one of my poems you become as docile as the words I toy with. In fact,
the mind is God or at least as silent and intense as God. The thought is
creation, the poet recreates. That's really it, sir, I am stuck with my
thoughts the way a garden is stuck with bad seeds. You may peer over
with friendly intrigue and lecture me on how horrid my garden will
look if I continue pouring water into them but like I said, they are stuck
with me. Do you think I enjoy viewing the mind as a cage? burying
seeds, sedulously. Sir, I'm fed up. No one should live like this; as poets
we must find ways to liberate ourselves. The pen understands this, it
respects it more than I. Nightly it waits like a mouth to swallow a storm
of thoughts then funnel out shrapnels of art. It is industrious, it has a
private festivity. And like the clever sheep, very keen, very loyal but also
insatiable with an ugly impulse. The pen doesn't try to justify anything
nor does it try to define. It's a sort of translation, fixing a language for
what I cannot name, the truths you shy from. You disagree with my
frankness, in fact you completely reject it. Withholding any interest for
the "dark thing" that "hinders" my work. But, sir, this is a part of me.
This dark thing removes me and has corrupted our mind. And if I do
not divulge and allow the pen to navigate, recover memories and fears
then I will become as broken, as lost as the bad seeds I tried to bury.
Sir, I must confront the mirror. It is a mad emptiness and the desire to
fulfil that are constantly fighting, how can I evade this? It is a product
of life. You may sneer at my nudity and question my pride; that's fine,
everything I do and say is executed with complete consciousness. I am
not begging for your approval, I doubt you'll recommend my work to
the most unversed reader. I only want you to realise that this pen won't
jeopardise my image, It will redefine it. Peeling it back like an onion,
I will have a truer purpose. You may not favour it but others will build
ideas, lay them out against mine. Others will reflect, feel heard and
familiarise. Even then you must consider the pen and the
sensationalised retelling of whatever feeling or event the poet has

attached themselves to. These words contain themselves independent of you and me. They perform a pulse the ear leans to, then swiftly kill themselves at the final breath of stanza. Sir, you must remember art is not reality. The poet encounters then ascends to an animate world that is in constant change and development, quietly shaped by the changes and development of said poet. I simply confess. It is your burden to uncover. Every sound, every clever sheep. Wool refashioned as clouds, random baas torn apart until the sheep become your own. Now you examine an illusion, a subtle reflection that frames your imagination not mine. Keep it! After all poetry is the deification of reality. If we destroy the illusion and put truth in its place we'd be charmless, uninspired, bored and blind as sheep.

Help Is Never Too Far

Reader, never feed into stigmas, It's okay to seek help. Whatever your situation may be, remember you are never alone. If you need an outlet, someone to turn to please contact one of the services listed below that'll guide you and give you the help you deserve.

Mental health services for men
Please reach out to...
-Give us a shout.org
-Mensmindsmatter.org
-uk.movember.com

Addiction/Substance abuse
Please reach out to...
-Priorygroup.com
-Thelaurelcentre.co.uk
-Recovery.org.uk

Services for Homelessness
Please reach out to...
-Emmnauelhouse.org.uk
-Crisis.org.uk
-SHP.org.uk

Single Parenthood
Please reach out to these teams
-Gingerbread.org.uk
-Homestart.org.uk
-Theurbangroup/themotherhoodgroup.org.uk

Suicide prevention/ Other Mental health services
Please reach out to these teams
-Womenatwish.org.uk
-Togetherwomen.org
- Papyrus-uk.org
-Youngminds.org.uk
-Samaritans.org | call **116-123**

Printed in Great Britain
by Amazon